Date: 10/7/15

MEASURING MANIA

MEASURING WEIGHT

by Beth Bence Reinke   illustrated by Kathleen Petelinsek

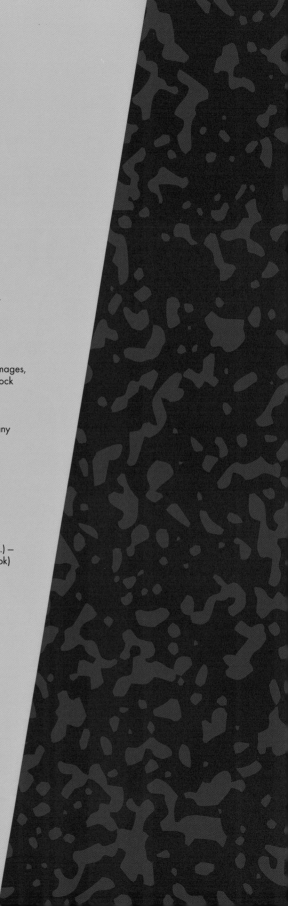

Published in the United States of America by Cherry Lake Publishing
Ann Arbor, Michigan
www.cherrylakepublishing.com

Consultants: Janice Bradley, PhD, Mathematically Connected Communities,
New Mexico State University; Marla Conn, ReadAbility, Inc.

Editorial direction: Red Line Editorial
Book design and illustration: The Design Lab

Photo credits: Oshchepkov Dmitry/Shutterstock Images, 4; Shutterstock Images,
5, 6; Minerva Studio/Shutterstock Images, 16; Olivier Le Moal/Shutterstock
Images, 17

Library of Congress Cataloging-in-Publication Data
Reinke, Beth Bence, author.
  Measuring weight / by Beth Bence Reinke.
      pages cm. — (Measuring mania)
  Audience: 5–8.
  Audience: K to grade 3.
  Includes bibliographical references and index.
  ISBN 978-1-62431-652-4 (hardcover) — ISBN 978-1-62431-679-1 (pbk.) —
ISBN 978-1-62431-706-4 (pdf) — ISBN 978-1-62431-733-0 (hosted ebook)
  1. Weight (Physics)–Measurement–Juvenile literature. I. Title.

  QC106.R45 2014
  530.8'1–dc23
                                                    2013029076

Cherry Lake Publishing would like to acknowledge
the work of The Partnership for 21st Century Skills.
Please visit www.p21.org for more information.

Printed in the United States of America
Corporate Graphics Inc.
January 2014

Table of Contents

CHAPTER ONE
What Is Weight?

Measure weight using a scale.

How much does Mia's kitten weigh? It's hard to tell by holding it. The vet uses a **scale** to measure the kitten's weight. Weight is how heavy something is.

The kitten's weight goes up as it grows. Mia gains weight as she grows, too. So do you!

It's fun to measure weight. We can weigh tiny things like paper clips. We can weigh big things like desks. You can even weigh your favorite grown-up.

Weigh yourself and a grown-up. What is the difference between your weights?

You can measure the weight of many things with a scale.

Which weighs more, a banana or an apple? How heavy is a puppy? How much does a letter weigh? You can find out. Let's measure weight!

To do the activities in this book, you will need:

- kitchen scale
- bathroom scale
- objects from around the house
- a pet, or an object from your home
- paper
- a pencil

Gather what you need.

CHAPTER TWO

Which Is Heavier?

If objects are close in weight, it's hard to tell which is heavier just by holding them.

Mia and Lee are playing at the park. They packed fruit for a snack. Which weighs more, the apple or the banana?

It's hard to guess by looking at them. Mia holds one fruit in each hand. It's still hard to tell which is heavier.

A **balance** compares weights of things. The heavier object goes down. The lighter object goes up. It balances if the two objects are equal. Now can you tell which fruit is heavier?

The balance shows which fruit is heavier.

A seesaw works like a balance. Lee's end goes down. That is because he is heavier than Mia.

Mia goes up. She is lighter than Lee. But we still do not know how much they weigh. We need a scale to measure weight.

Pretend You Are a Balance

Which things are heavier or lighter than a can of soup?

INSTRUCTIONS:
1. Gather items from your house. Some ideas are: banana, pen, book, flashlight, quarter, pair of jeans, hammer, and toothbrush.
2. Draw a line down the middle of a piece of paper. At the top, write "lighter" and "heavier."
3. Pick up each object. Guess whether it is lighter or heavier than the can of soup.
4. Now hold a small can of soup in one hand. Hold another object in the other hand. Is it lighter or heavier?
5. Write the object in the correct column.

To get a copy of this activity, visit www.cherrylakepublishing.com/activities.

Which is heavier, the banana or the can of soup?

CHAPTER THREE

Using Units

The scale measures how much the package weighs.

We use pounds or kilograms to measure heavy things. Pounds and kilograms are **units** of measure for weight. We measure people in pounds or kilograms.

Mia stops at the post office. She has a package for her grandmother and a letter to mail. The clerk weighs the package first.

She puts it on a scale. The package weighs three pounds (1.4 kilograms).

We can write pounds in a shorter way. The **abbreviation** for pounds is lb.

Heavier things like these are measured in pounds or kilograms.

Watermelons, puppies, and birthday cakes can all be measured in pounds or kilograms.

Other units of weight are ounces and grams. Lighter things are measured in ounces or grams. There are 16 ounces in a pound (0.5 kg).

The clerk weighs Mia's letter. It weighs one ounce. The short way to write ounces is oz. Sixteen letters would add up to one pound. Mia's letter is light. Can you think of other light objects?

Measure letters, bananas, and cupcakes in ounces or grams.

How Many Pounds Is the Puppy?

Lee's puppy will not sit still on a scale. But Lee found a way to measure him. You can try it, too.

INSTRUCTIONS:
1. Lee steps on a bathroom scale. He writes his weight on a piece of paper.
2. Then he weighs himself holding the puppy. He writes down that number.
3. Lee subtracts to find out how much his puppy weighs.
4. Do you have a pet to weigh? If not, find something else from around your house. Maybe a basket of clothes or a pair of boots? What else can you weigh?

To get a copy of this activity, visit www.cherrylakepublishing.com/activities.

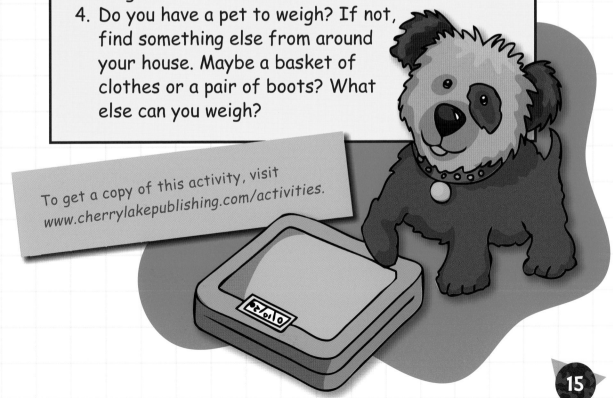

CHAPTER FOUR

Two Measuring Systems

Eight ounces plus eight ounces equals 16 ounces, or one pound (0.5 kg).

Lee and Mia shop at the market. Lee orders eight ounces (230 g) of yellow cheese. Mia asks for eight ounces of white cheese. That makes 16 ounces of cheese. That is the same as one pound (0.5 kg).

A worker slices the cheese. He weighs it on a scale. Lee counts 16 slices in one pound of cheese. Each slice weighs one ounce (28 g).

Ounces and pounds are units in the **U.S. customary system**. This system is one way we measure.

In the U.S. customary system, ounces and pounds measure weight.

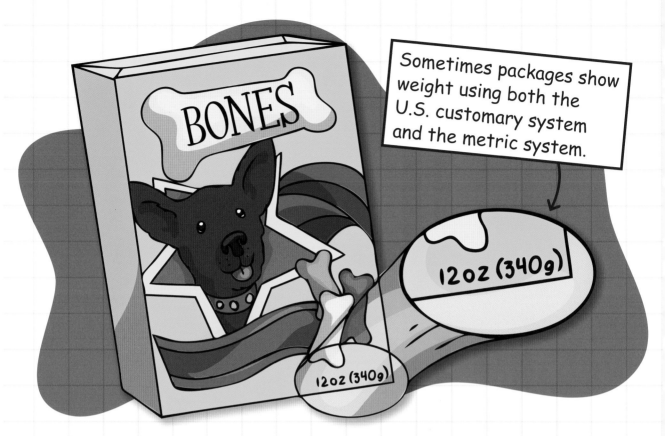

Sometimes packages show weight using both the U.S. customary system and the metric system.

12oz (340g)

12oz (340g)

We also measure with a second set of units. These units are the **metric system**. It uses grams and kilograms to measure weight. The short way to write grams is g. A paper clip weighs one gram. A kilogram is 1,000 grams. You can write kilograms as kg.

Most food packages show both ounces and grams. A gram is much smaller than an ounce. There are 28 grams in every ounce.

How Many Ounces?
How Many Grams?

You can weigh things in both grams and ounces. Let's try it!

INSTRUCTIONS:

1. Gather some light objects. Some ideas are: apple, spoon, phone, tissue box, car keys, salt shaker, hairbrush. You can find other objects, too.
2. Ask a grown-up how to use the kitchen scale. Where does it show weight in ounces? Where does it show weight in grams?
3. Put each object on a kitchen scale. Write down the weight in ounces.
4. Write down the weight in grams.
5. Arrange the items from heaviest to lightest.

To get a copy of this activity, visit
www.cherrylakepublishing.com/activities.

CHAPTER FIVE

You Can Measure Weight

Weigh a bowl of strawberries in pounds or kilograms. Weigh a letter in ounces or grams.

Every object has weight. We can measure weight using a scale.

How many pounds does a pillow weigh? How many ounces does today's mail weigh? Does a strawberry weigh more than a gram? You can find out!

Here are more fun ways to measure weight:

- Get on a seesaw with a friend. When you try to balance, who stays up? That person is lighter. Who stays down? That person is heavier. If the seesaw balances, you weigh the same.
- Use a kitchen scale to weigh pennies and dry pasta. How many pennies weigh one ounce (28 g)? How many pieces of pasta does it take to make three ounces (85 g)?
- Use a scale at the grocery store to weigh bananas. How many bananas are in one pound (0.5 kg)?
- Weigh a ball of clay on a kitchen scale. Then roll it into a log and weigh it again. Does it weigh the same?
- See if you can find out how much you weighed when you were born. Find some items from around your house. Weigh each item. See whether it weighs more or less than you did.

Glossary

abbreviation (uh-bree-vee-A-shun) a shorter form of a word

balance (BAL-ents) a tool used to compare weights

metric system (MEH-trik SIS-tum): a way to measure things based on the number ten; the gram is used to measure weight

scale (skal) a device used for weighing

units (YOO-nits) standard amounts used to measure things

U.S. customary system (YOO-es KUS-tuh-mer-ee SIS-tum) units of measurement typically used in the United States such as pounds, ounces, cups, quarts, miles, feet, and inches

For More Information

BOOKS

Cleary, Brian P. *On the Scale: A Weighty Tale*. Minneapolis, MN: Millbrook Press, 2010.

Karapetkova, Holly. *Pounds, Feet, and Inches*. Vero Beach, FL: Rourke Publishing, 2010.

Vogel, Julia. *Measuring Weight*. Mankato, MN: The Child's World, 2013.

WEB SITES

Matching Math: Weights
http://www.sheppardsoftware.com/mathgames/measurement /MeasurementOunces.htm
Match the pairs of pounds and ounces. Move to the next level when you get three correct.

Math is Fun: Discover Mass (Weight)
http://www.mathsisfun.com/activity/discover-mass.html
Weigh things from around your house. Make a list of the items from smallest to largest.

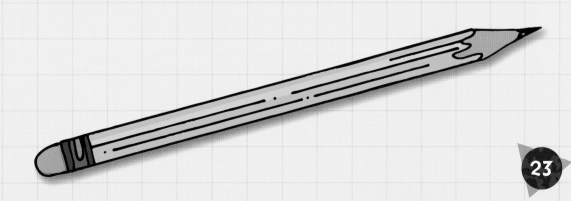

Index

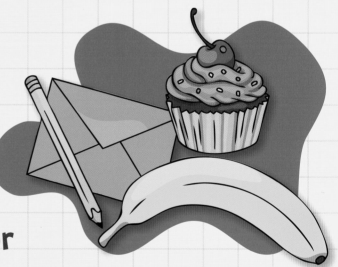

About the Author

Beth Bence Reinke has degrees in biology and nutrition. She is a registered dietitian, children's author, and a columnist for her favorite sport, NASCAR. When she goes grocery shopping, Beth thinks it is fun to weigh fruits and vegetables on the scale.